The Essentials

PERSONAL GOLF LESSONS

The Essentials

PETER D. SMITH

First published in Great Britain in 1994 by
ANAYA PUBLISHERS LTD
Strode House, 44-50 Osnaburgh Street, London NW1 3ND

Managing Editor Masterclass Design Limited
Photographer Maru Newcombe, Visions in Golf
Designer Roger Daniels
Illustrations Ken Lewis & Masterclass Design Studio

British Library Cataloguing in Publication Data

Smith, Peter
Personal Golf Lessons: Step-by-Step Guide
to Better Golf. – Essentials
I. Title
796.352

ISBN 1-85470-183-5

Typeset by Art Photoset Limited, Beaconsfield, Bucks.
Colour reproduction by J. Film Process, Singapore
Printed and bound in Singapore by
CS Graphics, Pte, Ltd.

Contents

Introduction

Golf is often made out to be a very difficult game. It is not. It is surprisingly easy once you fully understand a few basic facts and have mastered a few simple movements.

Many golf books try to make the game sound terribly complicated as well as highly technical, yet for the average golfer the game should be relatively simple and, above all, enjoyable. There is no magic formula that will instantly make you a better golfer, nor any well-guarded secrets known only to top professionals.

For many years now I have been fortunate to work with some of the world's top teaching and playing professionals. Over the years their expertise has helped countless golfers, of all standards, from beginners to champions.

In this series of lessons you, too, can benefit from their help and skill, as I have concentrated their teachings into this series of lessons. You will learn not only how easy golf could be, with a little effort on your part, but also how to put the skills you will acquire to good use on the course. The aim of this book is not to give you a perfect, mechanical swing. I won't try to teach you how to swing like Nick Faldo, simply because you are not Nick Faldo. You must learn to play to the best of *your* ability, using the skills you acquire in the best possible way, never taking risks but always playing shots you know you can hit.

The one aim of this book is to bring your scores down.

The newcomer to golf will find everything he or she needs to know about playing the game. The more experienced player too, who seriously wants to improve, will find it all in this series of lessons. I strongly urge everyone to read each section fully as even the more experienced golfer will find the revision of the essentials will cut several strokes off each round.

A quick note of apology to left-handed golfers. The photographs and text all refer to right-handed players and it is not possible within the space we have to repeat everything with the reversal of "left" and "right". I hope the inconvenience of reversing sides will not affect your enjoyment of, and benefit from, this course.

I may also have used the male gender "he" or "his" in certain places. To all the many fine women golfers there are, again my apologies for not always including "she" or "her". It is purely a matter of space, not a sign of any disrespect.

Learning from this book and then practising will bring your scores down. Scoring better makes your golf even more enjoyable.

Hit it Straight —
The Essential Ingredients

Every golfer wants to be able to hit the ball straight, or at least towards a definable target. To do so on a consistent basis, you will need the correct alignment, grip and stance.

Something like 80% of the faults in golf can be traced back to poor alignment, grip and set up, things you do before you even begin to swing the club. Get these right and you will have cut out 80% of your golfing problems.

I am going to show you the way to get into the best position to swing the club on a consistent basis and I shall deal with the process in exactly the same way as every professional would. Don't run away with the idea that this section is only for those who have never played golf, as it contains vital information for every golfer, of whatever standard. Even experienced golfers need to go back time and time again to the essentials, checking and rechecking them.

Only by getting these right will you be able to hit the ball well on a consistent basis. That will lower your scores substantially.

Alignment

What do you do when you want to hit a shot? Next time you are on the golf course make a mental note of your exact routine. I guarantee it is normally different from that of a professional.

What do they do? First, they look carefully at the lie of the ball, then calculate (normally with help from their caddy) how long the shot is to their target, whether that is the green or some other point on the course. They then decide what type of shot they need to hit, high, low, a fade or a draw; then and only then do they prepare to play the ball.

To do this they stand behind the ball, looking down the target line; then they move to the side of the ball, place the club head just behind the ball, adjusting it until it is square to the target line. Then they take their grip and get their stance right.

Just by reading this you can tell that the professionals take considerably longer than the average golfer at setting up before they hit a ball. The extra care they take is reflected in the greater accuracy they achieve. Forget the distance factor — professionals *do* hit the ball further than most club golfers. What is important is their degree of accuracy. How do they get it?

The answer is very simple. They line up better and take their grip very carefully as well as deciding exactly what type of shot they want to play.

In the example above — which you can watch on television or at any tournament — the sequence of events before a professional hits the ball is important and this is the way you must approach your golf if you are to play better. It is the only way to play.

It should become habit to align the club face and the body before taking the grip. Then, when the

---

Ian Woosnam proves that you don't have to be tall to power a golf ball.

grip is in place you are ready to play the shot. There is much you can do before you hit the ball, though not much after you have hit it to change its direction.

We start with the things you need to do **before** you swing.

You obviously need to know how long the shot is and what type of shot to play, but we shall return to that later. For now, just use a 7-iron and imagine you are faced with an easy, straight shot of about 135 yards, though if you hit a 7-iron less than this, don't worry.

Your first task, even before you take your grip, is to align the club face. If you are firing a gun or an arrow, playing snooker or bowling, you need to take aim first. It's the same with golf. Aim the club face in the right direction and you have a good chance of hitting the ball to your target.

In golf it has been shown that a 1° error in aligning the club will result in the ball being almost four yards off line at 200 yards. You can see from the illustration (below) that with a 3° error in alignment you would hit the ball 12 yards off

line. That could put it in the rough or in a bunker.

You will notice that the professionals stand behind the ball before they begin their alignment. They do this to be able to look from here directly down the line to their target. They often look for a small mark on the ground just ahead of the ball — a leaf or twig, or perhaps a patch of grass that is a slightly different colour — to use as a direction finder. This is perfectly legal under the rules of golf. Choose something no more than a yard or two away as it is easier to align yourself with something very close rather than 200 yards away. You cannot, though, place anything on your line to help you on the course, though on the practice area it may help you.

Once you can "see" an imaginary line from the ball to the target, place the club head on the ground a half inch behind the ball, with the

3°

A 3° error in alignment at address can cause you to hit the ball 12 yards off course. Be precise.

A novel way of seeing if the club face is perfectly aligned is to stick a tee-peg to the face. It should point at the heart of the ball and on to the target.

club face square to your target.

One novel little way of telling if the club is correctly aligned is to fix a tee peg to the face of the club, fastening the top end of the peg to the club with a re-useable adhesive. The tip of the tee-peg should then point straight at the middle of the ball. When the club head is in position move to the side of the ball to take up your stance.

For the purposes of this exercise we shall use extra clubs laid on the ground as aids to taking aim. On the practice ground use these to help you — it will quickly build up your confidence in lining up. The photographs show this clearly. It is normally easier to use the bottom groove on the club face as your guide.

Once the club face is aligned you are ready to get your body alignment correct. We shall, later in this course, deal with shaping shots which can entail altering the stance slightly, but for now our prime concern is to be able to hit the ball straight. You must, therefore, align your club absolutely square to the target.

On the ground parallel to the club marking the line from ball to target, lay another club, about three feet away from the first club. This will show you the line for your feet. Adjust it closer to the first club if needs be. You then align your shoulders.

Hold another club across your chest. It should be parallel to the club laying across your toes. If not, turn your shoulders very slightly until it is.

You are now totally square to the target and thus perfectly aligned. You are now halfway to hitting the ball straight.

Lay some clubs on the ground to help you with your alignment. This will help train your eyes, making it easier for you once you are out on the course.

Hold another club across your shoulders, parallel to the club across your feet. You are now aligned.

11

Your Grip

Once the club face and body are aligned you take your grip, though be careful not to move the club head out of position.

The most widely used grip is the one popularised by the great Jersey professional Harry Vardon. Although he did not invent the grip his success in winning the British Open six times between 1896 and 1914 (a feat never equalled) focused attention on his technique. Consequently most golfers adapted their grips to the one he used. It is a tribute to that fine man that it has become known as the **Vardon grip**.

Basically it has the little finger of the right hand overlapping the valley formed by the index and middle fingers of the left hand, as the photograph clearly shows. It is also often referred to as the overlapping grip.

There are a couple of variations which have evolved over the years. One, known as the "interlocking" grip, has been very successfully used by Jack Nicklaus and has the little finger of the right hand interlocking with the index finger of the left. It can be of benefit to players with short fingers. The great Ben Hogan used a similar grip.

The other grip is the ten finger grip, sometimes referred to as the "baseball" grip, and this is particularly useful if you have small hands. Many younger golfers and women use this grip. With this grip it is particularly important to ensure that there is no gap between the two hands — they must form a single unit.

Whichever grip you may feel comfortable with, the point to understand is that the hands must form a single unit — if they are not firmly connected they may work independently, creating all sorts of problems in your swing.

Take your grip with your left hand first. The club should lay across your left hand from the "heel" — the pad opposite the base of the thumb -— to the first joint of the index finger. Leave about half an inch of the club overhanging the end of the hand; this helps you to control the club better and will stop your glove wearing out.

The fingers then close around the club. With the club head on the ground the left thumb should be very slightly to the right of the centre of the shaft. If you have your thumb straight down the centre of the shaft, loosen the grip, turn your hand very slightly to the right and re-grip. You should be able to see two knuckles on your left hand but as this can sometimes be difficult when looking down you may find it easier to hold the club upright, as shown. Make sure you put it down square though, rechecking your aim. Another good check point is that, if you have gripped correctly, the back of your left hand (use the logo on the glove as a guide) should be aiming directly towards the target.

You should also be able to see that the two middle fingers are just touching the pad at the base of the thumb. If they don't touch you might need to have smaller grips fitted to your clubs, or you should grip down the shaft a little until they do just touch. If they overlap the thumb pad you might need larger grips fitted. Ask your club professional to check this for you if you are in doubt.

The right hand is then placed in position. Here, the club does not lie across the hand so much but is

Right For people with smaller hands the ten finger grip can be suitable, but the hands must be kept close together.

Below The most widely used grip is the Vardon, or overlapping grip.

Below right The interlocking grip has been used by Nicklaus to great effect.

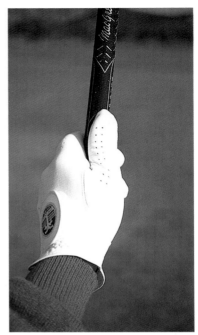

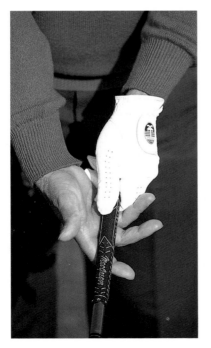

gripped more at the point where the fingers meet the palm, right at the base of the fingers. You must never grip the club in the palm of your right hand.

Wrap the middle two fingers around the club with the little finger overlapping the valley between the index and middle fingers of the left hand. The index finger of the right hand then wraps around the club but with a small gap between it and the middle finger. This is often referred to as the "trigger".

The joint of the right thumb and first finger squeezes together rather than being wide open.

If you use a grip other than the Vardon the only difference from any of the above is the position of the little finger of the right hand. Apart from that, nothing else in the entire set up or swing changes.

Your hands should now fit together snugly as a single unit. The left thumb is covered by the thumb pad of the right hand and, importantly, the "V"s formed by the joints of thumbs and first fingers should be pointing in the same direction, ideally towards a point midway between the chin and the right shoulder.

Many newcomers to golf — and a fairly large number of those who have been playing the game for several years — have what is termed a "strong" grip, the hands turned too far to the right. This can often cause a hook, unlike the "weak" grip where, with the hands turned too far left, you risk slicing the ball.

You can see these two positions, slightly exaggerated, over the page. Check your grip position in a mirror at home, where you can also practise taking your grip and setting your aim.

Opposite, top left Leave about half an inch overlapping the hand. This gives more control.

Opposite, top right It is easier to see the two knuckles on your left hand if you hold the club upright in front of you.

Above Your two middle fingers should just touch the thumb pad as you grip the club. If they don't, ask your professional to check your grip size.

Opposite, bottom left The right hand grip is more in the fingers, with the index finger forming a trigger to give more control.

Opposite, bottom right Both the "V"s formed by the thumb and first finger should be pointing at the same spot, between the chin and right shoulder.

This is a weak grip, the "V"s pointing at the left shoulder. This will cause a slice.

This is a strong grip, the "V"s pointing beyond the right shoulder. This would lead to a hook.

A tiny word too, about grip pressure. You need to hold the club firmly, so that it doesn't slip out of your hands as you swing, but you should not hold it so tight that you are strangling it. Hold it with the same pressure that you would use if you were holding a young child or a cat.

Far too many players grip the club as if they were about to strangle it. This is wrong and will result in poor shots. You do, of course, need to maintain control over the club and can't let it fly out of your hands once you swing it, but do relax your grip. If you ever want to check that you are not gripping too tightly, completely slacken off the pressure without removing your hands from the club, then slightly tighten them again. Feel that your hands are more relaxed.

The grip is something that needs fine tuning on a regular basis just like a high performance motor car. Having the grip slightly wrong will make all the difference between a good shot and a poor one. Take the time to get it right and constantly recheck it.

Whenever you hit a bad shot, go back to your grip and look at it carefully. There's a fifty-fifty chance that the shot was poor because of a faulty grip position. You will see professionals, whenever they hit a bad shot, replaying the shot — without a ball — to try to figure out what they did wrong. This is good practice, provided you know what you are looking for.

Opposite right Sandy Lyle went through a poor patch before bouncing back. If your game goes wrong come back to the essentials and work on getting them right.

Every golfer will find that their game goes slightly awry from time to time with shots being hit that are just not up to their normal standard. Every golfer goes through a poor patch now and again — even professionals; just think of Sandy Lyle who won the British Open and the US Masters, then had a couple of years of sheer misery before bouncing back. If you do have an off day don't go for drastic cures or try to change your swing. Go back to the beginning. Check your grip. Take your left hand grip and hold the club upright to see if you can see two knuckles.

Check that your "V"s are pointing to the correct place. Check that both your hands are perfectly aligned and that one is not drifting very slightly to one side.

Check your alignment too, to make sure you have been standing square to your target. Look in particular at your shoulder line as the shoulders and feet are often not quite properly aligned.

It pays to check and re-check the alignment and the grip. It takes very little time and you really should do it before every shot, just like the professionals.

The club hits the ball just before the bottom of the swing arc, which is why the ball will rise and spin.

If they consider it so important, even with their superior ball striking ability, it must be. You will play a better class of golf by following their example.

Never be afraid to return to this section — it is not a sign of weakness to go back to the essentials, but a sign of strength. If your grip and alignment are fine-tuned regularly, then you know that you will be able to play better golf more often. That must be worthwhile.

Addressing the Ball
The alignment and grip are the most important parts of the essential ingredients. We now move on to the address position, including the stance and ball position.

For an iron shot the ball should be played fractionally before the point where your swing reaches its nadir, with the club face square to the target.

The swing should bring the club head back into the same position every time. The thing to remember is that at impact the position of the club head should be exactly the same as it was at address. The ball needs to be in a position where you can comfortably get the club head square at the bottom of the swing arc every time.

Finding the exact ball position to suit your swing will take some time, as it varies from person to person, as does the swing itself.

Many teachers insist that the ball should be midway between the instep of your left foot and the centre of your stance, but I have to disagree with them slightly and tell you that it varies according to the shot and according to your swing pattern. That is dependent, to a degree, on your height and build.

Other teachers suggest that the

ball should be moved slightly back as the length of the shot decreases, the ball being furthest forward for the driver and furthest back for the wedge. There is far more validity to this suggestion and I would recommend you adopt this method,

I think you should slightly alter the ball position according to your shot. Obviously the longest club — the driver — puts the ball furthest from you, but it should also be further forward in your stance. Adjust the ball position according to *your* swing.

but only if it suits your swing pattern. I would stress that this holds good for normal shots from the fairway — at present we are not dealing with any problem shots or shots you wish to shape. Those we shall deal with later.

If you find you are topping the ball, or slicing it, try adjusting the position of your feet so that the ball is more in the centre of your stance. I would emphasise that this is for an iron shot; it changes slightly with a tee shot, but that is something we shall deal with later.

It is fairly obvious that, to hit a golf ball well, you need to be well balanced. In general your feet should be about shoulder width apart, wide enough to ensure you maintain your balance but not that wide that you risk swaying.

One quick way to find this is by walking! Suddenly stop, one foot a pace ahead of the other. Turn on your heels so that you are facing the front. Your feet are now the natural distance apart for you to make an athletic swing whilst remaining well balanced. Nature does it for you!

With your feet too far apart you will restrict your turn, tending to sway more. Put them too close together and you might lose your balance as you swing. Experiment with it until you feel comfortable.

One thing that newcomers find difficult is standing the correct distance from the ball. To some degree you will find this by trial and error, but if you stand too close to the ball you will swing more upright and possibly slice the ball; standing too far will cause you to swing flat and that could lead to a hook.

You can check by releasing one hand from the grip at

Above and above right To find the correct feet width for you, try walking! Stop, turn on your heels and you have the perfect stance, compliments of nature!

Opposite, far right The club should not be held too close to the body — about a hand's width from the thighs is ideal.

Right As you address the ball make sure that your right arm is not too far out in front of you as that will push your shoulders into an open position and cause a slice. Relax the right elbow more, holding it closer in to the side of the body.

address and placing it between
the club and your left thigh. This is
a generalisation — don't measure
it to the nearest millimetre! Feel
comfortable.

One other vitally important
ingredient in a good set up
position is the way the arms hang
when you are gripping the club.
I see a great number of golfers who
stand with their right arm too
straight and held out too much in
front. This pushes the right
shoulder too high and forward,
opening the shoulder line to the
target and possibly causing a
slice.

Good golfers stand with their
right arm slightly more folded, and
almost held in against their side.
The fold of the right elbow — not
the elbow bone itself — should be
pointing about 45° left and
forward, not directly left. This set
up will help you to draw the ball,
making you a better golfer.

Do beware, though, of holding it
too close in to the body as that will
restrict the flowing movement of
the swing and you will lose the
width of the swing.

The body at address can almost
be divided into three; from the
head to the hips; hips to knees;
and knees to feet. Ideally, each of
these three sections should be a
straight line, but as we are not stick
men this is not literally possible.
Make sure you bend from the hips,
not the waist.

Try to keep your spine as
straight as possible, without
becoming so rigid that you cannot
turn. Your knees need to be flexed
slightly. A large number of
beginners stand with their legs too
straight. This restricts the turn. You
must remember to be athletically
poised — not a statue.

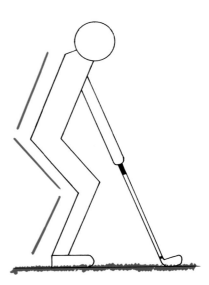

Try to keep your spine fairly straight,
though not wooden. Try this simple
exercise to see how upright you stand.

You will also see a number of
golfers with their heads too low,
their chins virtually resting on their
chests. In this position the left
shoulder, as you turn on the back
swing, will knock the head out of
position, and as one of the
important points in golf is to keep
the head fairly still, this immediately puts you at a disadvantage.
Your head needs to be held erect
enough for your arms to be able to
swing through unhindered, and for
your head to be able to remain
fairly still. Too many golfers, having
been urged to "keep your head
down", do so at address.

Your chin must be comfortably
held up as it is in normal, everyday
life. Don't let it droop, but don't
hold your nose in the air.

Never drop your head too much onto
your chest as this will restrict your
body turn.

The Swing

Now that we are fully in position, athletically poised and perfectly aligned, the next thing to do is to swing the club and hit the ball. The swing is often described in parts — the take-away, the back swing, the downswing and the follow-through.

Whilst it makes it more understandable to describe each part in detail, you must remember, when you come to swing the club, that it is just one flowing movement. For example, the take-away is merely the first part of the back swing; at the top of the back swing there is no pause before you launch into the downswing. Indeed, at the top of the back swing there is, in good players, a minute fraction of a second when the club is still being swung back, yet the body has started the downswing.

Don't let any of this confuse you. You will see how natural it is as we proceed. There are a couple of points about the swing you must understand. First, the back swing is a coiling motion, like winding up a spring. Think of one of those children's toys where you wind up a key and then release the toy, which scuttles away under its own power. The swing is like that. As you wind it up the key stays at the centre of the spring. The spring winds round the key. So it is with winding up the golf swing. The spring (in this case the arms and club) winds round the key (the body's pivot). A lot of golfers let the "key" move to one side — that is definitely wrong as we shall see a little later.

The body's pivot is an imaginary line from the head to a point midway between the feet. Basically it's a plumb-line from the head. Keeping your head firmly in place on the back swing will make you a much better golfer. The right leg plays a major part in this as we shall see, but remember — the spring coils round the key.

Before we begin swinging the club I want you to try a couple of very simple exercises.

Stand perfectly upright, your legs straight and your feet apart. Hold a golf club across your chest with your arms folded. Without moving your feet, but keeping your head as still as you can, turn your shoulders to the right until the club is pointing straight out in front of you. Hold that position and you should feel a stretching sensation in the back muscles.

Now turn to the left as far as you can go, though this time you can move your head so that you finish with your head and upper body facing the left. Also kick your right knee round so that it, too, is pointing at the target. Repeat the exercise half a dozen times until it feels fairly natural.

One more exercise before we swing the club. Place a golf umbrella in the ground and, as you stand, have your right leg pressed up against it. Now repeat the turning exercises a dozen times, stretching round to the right as far as you can go, but make sure you do not knock the umbrella out of the way. If you do knock it over you have swayed as you have turned right. That is one of the biggest faults in golf and one you must avoid at all costs.

Cast your mind back a few paragraphs to the child's toy and the

The swing is one smoothly flowing movement as Greg Norman demonstrates here effortlessly.

25

Above and left Practise the golf turn by holding a club across your chest and turning as far to the right as you can, really stretching your back muscles, then turn to the left, turning to face the target as you do so. This is a wonderful exercise at the start of your round of golf.

Right To avoid swaying on the back swing place an umbrella in the ground by your right knee and swing; you should not knock it out of position.

key. I said that the spring coils around the key, but that the key does not move out of position. The key is the body's pivot and the right knee is a major part of that pivot. You really must work very hard on keeping that right knee firm in the back swing. Not straight, firm. It is something we shall return to, but I would strongly recommend that, every time you play golf, or practise, you spend a couple of minutes doing this turning exercise. First it loosens the muscles and helps you stretch; second it reminds your muscles how to coil to build up the power of the golf swing.

Now back to the swing itself, with the club in position.

The first part of the swing is the take-away — that is, moving the club back from the ball as we begin to rotate the shoulders. There is a considerable amount of confusion over the take-away, mainly, I think, because too many golfers have, in the past, been told that it must be a "straight" take-away. It is not.

I am going to suggest here that you hold a club and, as you read this, enact the swing in very slow motion. It will help you to understand better the various ingredients of the swing that we have to put together later.

The swing begins with the arms and wrists held firmly — again, not rigid but firm enough that the "Y" formed by the club and arms does not change its shape for the first part of the back swing. The back swing starts with the shoulders rotating. Feel that you are pulling the right shoulder backwards. This automatically pulls the arms round and the club will follow. Be careful that you rotate the shoulders round the pivot — that plumb-line down the back of the spine — rather than swaying to one side.

You must also avoid "picking the club up" on the take-away. That will produce too steep a swing, with a loss of power and direction in the shot.

A number of players, having in mind the "straight take-away" idea that has been mentioned in golf books before, move the club head back in a straight line. This can lead to what is known as an out-to-in swing on the way back down, the club head approaching the ball from outside the line.

As the right shoulder rotates backwards the arms follow it, bringing the club up and round. Keep the wrists firm at this point so that, if you suddenly stopped the swing, put the club head back on the ground where it is and turned your feet, you would be back in your address position.

Continue turning the shoulders. As you do so the arms are pulled back, as is the club. At some point the wrists will "cock", or hinge, but they will do this of their own accord, without you even having to think about it. A lot of golfers worry about getting the wrist-cock correct. Forget it — it happens on its own. Don't try to do it — don't try to stop it. Just swing the club.

As you swing the club back, your head should stay fairly still. I suggest, though, that you focus one eye firmly on the back of the ball, as doing something physical is simpler than thinking about something. Also, try to keep your left arm fairly straight so that you are extending the arc of the swing. That helps build up power.

Do make sure that you really turn your shoulders as far round as they can go, at least 90°, so that

The Swing Plane

To understand the swing plane better it might help to draw an imaginary line from the ball to the target, taking that line further back a couple of yards as well. You are standing inside that line and as you swing back the club will move inside that line. The downswing then brings the club down to the ball inside the line. At impact the club must be right on that line, to hit the ball squarely. It then moves along the line momentarily as it hits the ball before moving back inside the line again. This is referred to as an "in-to-in" swing pattern.

Some players swing the club outside the line on the way down to the ball, leading to either a slice or a pull left. This is called an "out-to-in" swing. There is also an "in-to-out" swing where the club approaches the ball from inside the line but then carries on going across it to outside. This can cause either a nasty hook or, more likely, a straight push to the right. Remember the "in-to-in" swing pattern and you will end up hitting more shots straight.

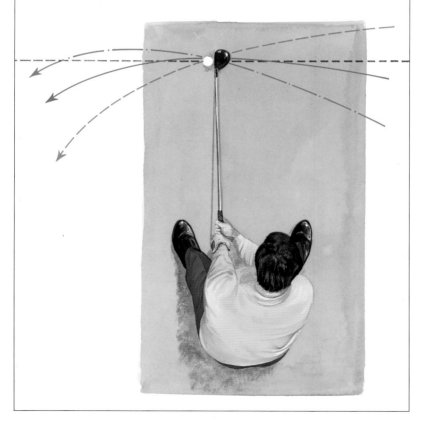

your back is facing the target. Keep one eye focused on the ball.

A number of golfers raise their left heel at this point. To be a really good golfer you should try to keep the left heel firmly on the ground, only rolling the left foot slightly onto its instep. If you find that difficult raise it only very slightly.

Your right leg must stay firmly flexed, just as at address. From that position, all it does is twist from the hip. You must not let it sway to one side or you will pull the entire pivot out of line. Remember our umbrella.

Don't, however, go the other way and let your right leg sway away from the umbrella. This is known as a reverse pivot and it, too, will cause you some major problems.

At the top of the back swing you should be feeling a stretching sensation in your back muscles. Your shoulders should have turned well through 90°, your hips about 45°, and the club should be virtually horizontal and pointing straight down your target line. You can't always see this for yourself, so get a friend to help you check it.

Make sure, though, that they fully understand what they are supposed to be looking for. Advice from some golfers, friendly and well meant though it might be, can sometimes make a poor position

At the top of the back swing the shoulders must have turned through 90° so that your back is facing the target. Keep your left heel on the ground.

The view from the front shows that the shoulders have completed their 90° turn, the head is still above the back of the ball and the hips have not swayed to the right.

worse. The best thing to do is either to use a mirror or to ask a golf professional to have a quick look at you.

Now for the downswing, and there is an ongoing debate about what starts this. Some say the legs, some the arms, some the shoulders; others the hips. With our wind-up toy, releasing the key and placing it on the floor starts the thing in motion.

The human body is not quite as mechanical as that and we need to do something to kick-start the downswing. As I said, opinions vary but the majority of more experienced golf professionals now suggest that it is the lateral movement of the body weight towards the target that drives the swing. At the same time the hands pull down hard on the club and the hips turn out of the way to make room for the club to swing through. It is, though, all a matter of transferring the weight.

Think of a glass of water. If you hold it still but then suddenly move it to one side (the back swing), the water changes its level in the glass but would then find its natural level again if held still.

If you then swing it the other way (transferring the weight on the downswing) the water resists but then catches up again, coming back to level. The body weight does

The turning of the hips, together with the lateral movement of the body weight to the left, kicks the downswing. The arms pull down hard on the club. At this point the hands are ahead of the club head.

Fractionally after impact you can see how the right arm has straightened, the hips have moved out of the way and the body weight has hit through the ball and is still transferring to the left. The head has stayed over the back of the ball until after impact.

A moment before impact the hands are still working overtime to get the club head back to that square position. You must, though, never try to hit "late". I would suggest, on the contrary, you try to hit early, making sure your left arm is straight at impact, as it was at address.

At impact the arms and hands have returned the club to its square position, seen better in this picture with the driver.

Drive the club head through after impact, rather than trying to decelerate it quickly. As you finish you should be facing the target, your right knee having kicked round and your weight perfectly balanced.

exactly the same in the swing.

The back swing pulls the weight to one side of the body — though it turns rather than sways. Then it transfers to the left as you swing. The important point is that you move the glass first — the water catches up with it because at first it resists by flowing up the right side of the glass before the force of the glass moving makes it catch up and settle to level again.

Impact

Let's look, now, at what position we want to create at impact. The club face needs to be perfectly square to the target. To achieve that the arms need to swing down. To make room for them the hips need to be moved out of the way.

Let's start with the hips. At the top of the back swing they have turned through about 45°.

They are, though, still perfectly positioned over the pivot line. Although I have warned you against swaying on the back swing, the first movement on the downswing is a sideways sway of the hips to the left. They begin turning at the same time.

As this lateral movement of the hips towards the target begins you must pull the club down with your hands, just as if you were pulling down on a bell rope. You will remember that we have tried to keep the left arm as straight as possible throughout the back swing. You want to try to keep it fairly straight coming down as well. This increases the width of the swing arc and will give you more power.

As the arms begin pulling the club down your hips will rotate towards the left, the weight moving onto your left foot. Don't try to do anything unnatural here — concentrate on moving the hips out of the way and keeping the left arm straight: the rest will follow.

As you approach the impact position your hips are ahead of the ball, yet your head is still behind it. Be careful, as you move your hips laterally, that you do not pull your head out of position. It must not move. Concentrate on focusing one eye on the ball and the head will remain fairly still.

At impact itself the biggest single fault of less experienced golfers is to have the club head trailing behind the hands. Look carefully at the photograph and you will see that the straight line we had at address, from the club head up through the shaft and right arm to the shoulder is almost exactly repeated at impact. This picture also clearly shows how the hips have moved out of position, but look very closely at the position of the hands. Compare it with the photograph where we are halfway down before impact. In that photograph the hands are still pulling the club down and the wrists are still cocked — there is no straight line from the shoulder to the club head.

Somewhere between the two positions shown, the wrists have to straighten the club to replicate the straight line we had at address. Inexperienced golfers can lack the strength and technique to do that, often leaving the club behind. That can cause a slice or a push right.

The wrists have to work overtime here to get the straight line at impact. You will recall that we also saw that at impact the club face has to be in the same position as it was at address — that is, square to the target. This is

possibly the hardest part of the golf swing and you will not master it immediately.

We shall go back over this in a few minutes.

After impact comes the matter of the follow-through and once again this is an often neglected part of the swing. Although you can do nothing after impact to change the direction of the ball you must be aware that the swing is one flowing movement and if you have performed the parts before impact correctly, you will finish in a certain position. If you finish out of position you will know that, somewhere in the swing, you have done something wrong. The ball will also tell you what you have done wrong by the way it flies (or doesn't!). In the advanced section later in this course we shall be looking at how you can use the flight of the ball to tell you what you have done wrong.

Getting to a good follow-through position is just proof that you have kept accelerating the club head through the impact zone, thus putting all your power into the shot. Had you slowed the club down before impact you would not have hit it hard enough. At impact the club head needs to be travelling at its maximum speed.

From the top of the back swing the club head picks up speed, being at maximum speed as it hits the ball. Thereafter it continues up into the finish position, but it must not be slowed down too early.

At impact the left arm is straight, but the right is slightly flexed at the elbow. Just after impact the right arm, too, straightens as the right hand begins rolling over the top of the left.

This is a difficult part to get right

but it is largely the way the hands work which allows professionals to hit the ball further.

We shall come back to this later in the course as we move on to discuss more advanced techniques, but if you can understand it here you will be on the right track.

One more thing you should do is to drive the club head down the target line after impact — just one more reason why you should not slow the club down at impact.

Imagine that you have a further target just a couple of feet ahead of the ball and that you need to hit this with the club head. As you can

To help you think about driving the club head through the impact zone imagine you have another club ahead of you, set into the ground. Your aim should be to hit the grip of this club as you continue your follow-through.

see from the photograph I have set another club in the ground. My aim, after having hit the ball, is to hit towards the grip of this club with the club I am swinging. That will help ensure that I am swinging straight down the line at impact, rather than aiming the club face off outside the line, or too far inside.

You almost get the impression,

with this exercise, that you are steering the shot. That is a good feeling to acquire and will result in you hitting a much higher proportion of straight shots.

After impact the body keeps rotating so that you finish facing the target. Your right knee has kicked round completely and your right foot is on tip-toe. Do make sure that when the right knee kicks it moves round to the left, towards the target, not out in front of you. That is a fault of many golfers and will lead to a loss of power. Whilst dealing with the legs, try to finish with your left leg reasonably straight; don't let it collapse.

You should finish upright and perfectly balanced.

Finally, a word about the speed of the swing. Bobby Jones once said that nobody has ever swung a club too slowly. Although he said that over 70 years ago when clubs were made of different material, it still holds good today. Most golfers try to swing too quickly, with a resultant loss of control. There is no definite speed at which you should swing. Everyone is different, some can swing much faster than others. Vijay Singh, the top Fijian golfer, swings the club through faster than Concorde. He can, though, control it.

Today's top professionals swing the club, from start to finish, in about 0.8 of a second. From the start of the take-away to the top of the back swing is about 0.6 of a second; from the top of the back

swing to the finish is about 0.2 of a second. You can clearly see from this just how important it is to have a slow, controlled back swing. The club does, after all, come to a stop at the top of the back swing before it begins its journey down towards the ball, so there really is no point in swinging back fast.

You and I cannot, and should not, swing the club too fast. To help you with your swing rhythm, particularly at the start of a round or practice session, swing two clubs together. This does two things. It helps to establish a good swing rhythm; and it also ensures that you get your hands moving well ahead of the club head on the downswing as well as forcing you to move your hips forward and out of the way as you swing through.

A lot of golfers think they will hit the ball further if they swing faster. Most of them won't. But try it next time you are at the driving range. Swing as fast as you possibly can. The results will probably be horrible, so you can quickly go back to establishing a **smooth** swing.

This, then, is the swing technique. It may sound a lot to learn for something that happens in less than a second, but it is the only thing you do in golf so you should take the time to learn it.

Nobody gets it right every time but if you understand what you should be doing and why, it might make it easier to get it right on a consistent basis.

Don't give up if, having read this, you go out and find that the ball is not going exactly where you planned. It takes the three "P"s — perseverance, practice and patience. But everyone can do it.

Vijay Singh, the popular Fijian golfer, has one of the fastest swings on the European Tour. If you ever get the chance, watch him, but don't try to mimic him or you might lose control. Swing to the best of *your* ability.

Hit the Green!

Many golfers fail to get the ball onto the green with their second shot on some par-4s, either because they lack length on their tee shot or from the fairway, or because their approach shot is a little wayward.

To make par they need to get the ball very close with the next shot. This is why the short game is such a vital part of golf. I want to show you how to get the ball safely on the green every time on those short shots.

We have so far looked at the alignment, set up, grip and swing. We have been using something like a 7-iron for these exercises and I suggest that, for what we shall do now, you use the same club.

In a round of golf there are eighteen holes, four of which are normally par-3s. Of the remaining fourteen only about ten or twelve will require a driver. If your first aim in golf is to score 90 on a regular basis — and let me put that in its proper perspective by telling you that 80% of all golfers in the world never regularly score less than 90 — you will only use the driver about a dozen times in a round. By the way, break 90 regularly and you will be in the top 20% of golfers in the world. Think about it.

Although we are using only one club at the moment, all the short irons are used in basically the same way. In an average round of golf,

60% of all shots are played within 100 yards of the pin, so you will probably use the short irons about thirty-five times.

The short game requires pinpoint accuracy and perfectly struck shots every time. I am going to teach you two things. First, in this part of the course, how to get the ball safely on the green nine times out of ten, whether there are bunkers, lakes or anything else in the way.

In the second part of this course I shall show you how to hit close to the pin whenever it is reasonably safe to do so but, above all, to play within your capabilities. You will always be playing the nine-times-out-of-ten shot, not the shot of a lifetime.

We are going to start with a little chip shot, the sort we might encounter if we were about 40 yards from the flag with no bunkers or other hazards in the way. Once that is mastered we can move back to hit longer shots.

If you can learn to hit shots accurately 40 yards, you can hit them accurately 240 yards. A long shot is the same as a short shot with one variation — the arc of the swing is wider, not because you swing the club differently but because the club shaft is longer. If you can control the club head on a short shot you will be able to control it on a long shot.

For this exercise you will need to be at the practice area of your local golf course. Stick an umbrella in the ground about 60 yards away. For a moment I want you to put the club aside, choose a new target about 20 yards away — I marked

Nick Faldo shows supreme control on this short shot to the green. It is the ability to get the ball close to the pin from these situations which sets up birdie opportunities — or saves a par!

Have two targets — one about 20 yards away, the other at about 60 yards. Once you have mastered these exercises hit balls to each target alternately.

Throw a ball to a target 20 yards away. You will note that the "follow-through" is longer than the "back swing". Note also how the ball rolls towards the target once it lands.

As you swing the club you will notice a ratio of about 45/55 in the lengths of the back swing and follow-through. To increase the length of shot increase the length of swing.

that one with the umbrella and the 60 yard target with a flag, as they show better in photographs — and throw a few golf balls underarm to land by it. Try six or seven until you can get them to land fairly close — within about two feet. As you throw them make a mental note of how far you draw your arm back and how far forward your arm goes as you release the ball.

Chances are the ratio back to through was in the region of 45:55. Now take the club again and try to swing it through with the same ratio — that is about 45% back; 55% through. You don't need to hit the ball yet.

At the finish the club should just come up to the horizontal. This is not a full "wind-it-round-your-neck" finish, but just a little push forward of the club, not much more than for a long putt, really.

Now let's set up correctly and play the shot, to the further target. Have the ball in the middle of your stance and stand slightly open to the target. We do this because, on a short shot, you do not have the same lower body movement as on a full shot. Therefore the hips do not rotate in the back swing by much, nor do they move out of the way on the downswing.

To compensate for this we need to move them out of the way in the beginning or we risk knocking our arms against our left leg as we play the shot. The other point about standing open to the target is that it restricts your back swing and, as we have seen, we only want a very short back swing.

An important note here about the ball being in the middle of the stance. In our first section I emphasised the importance of getting the right ball position to suit your swing, suggesting that, to begin with, you had the ball in the middle of your stance and that you stand square to the target.

When we open the stance (don't confuse this with having your feet wider apart — we are talking about turning the body slightly to the left of the target) the ball immediately appears to be further back in the stance. This is particularly so on short shots and in some bunkers where we need to stand quite open to the target. Some golf books suggest that, on a short shot, the ball should be opposite your left instep. If you took this literally, aligning your body first and then positioning the ball, you would, in reality, have the ball so far forward that it would be way outside your left foot and very difficult to play.

Stand square first, get the ball positioned correctly to your **square** stance, then change the body alignment. The ball will **appear** to move **back** in your stance — that is exactly what you want. For a shot this short your feet should be fairly close together, but maintain your balance.

Because of this stance and ball position your hands will be slightly ahead of the ball, so that your wrists are already slightly hinged. The line from your left shoulder down through your arm and the club shaft should be virtually straight, though don't hold your arm ram-rod stiff, or get into an uncomfortable position. You must feel relaxed, not tense.

As you swing the club back your

If you stand square with the ball centrally in your stance, but then turn so that you are standing open, the ball appears to move back in your stance. Take a square stance first.

The ball here is fairly central, but note how there is an almost straight line from the left shoulder to the club head. You need the same straight line at impact.

This is not quite a full back swing, the hands only just reaching the shoulders. The shoulders must turn, however.

At impact there is a straight line again from the left shoulder to the club head.

You should finish with the arms fairly straight in front of you. This helps restrict the length of shot. You do not need a full follow-through as this is not a full shot.

wrists will cock slightly, but do guard against picking the club up steeply. Your wrists should stay reasonably firm so that the angle between your left arm and the shaft does not alter too much.

You also have to realise that the club head needs to be accelerating into the ball so you need to swing it back far enough to be able to produce enough speed at impact. Getting to know the exact length of back swing will take some time and practice.

Having decided on the length of swing you need, and keeping your wrists firmly held in that pre-set position relative to the arms, swing the club back and through. The slow back swing will help you to accelerate the club head through impact. That is vital on long shots but it is probably more important on short shots where you really must push the club head through impact, not slowing down at all. Remember, also, that you have 45% of your swing back, 55% through. To get the club that far through you *have* to accelerate from the top of the back swing.

As you come through impact keep the club head accelerating but keep the same angle between arm and shaft that you had at address. You should finish with the left arm and shaft in a straight line, as the photograph clearly shows. If that line is broken it is because you have flicked at the ball rather than hitting through it. You must get the feeling, in much of golf and particularly on short shots, that you are dragging the club head through with your left arm and wrist. To really understand this feeling you should practise short shots just using your left arm and hand. You will have to keep the left wrist fairly

firm to control the club head and your arm must stay firm if you are to hit the ball. Try it. Hitting 30 balls one-handed will help you to understand how the wrists work.

If you just take the club back and then limply swing it at the ball you will merely bounce the ball forward ineffectively. It must be a crisp shot into the back of the ball, with a longer follow-through than back swing. To control the shot you must keep the wrists firm, which will keep the club face on line and result in the shot going to the target. If you are not hitting it straight it is because you have changed the alignment of the club face between address and impact.

This is a very gentle shot, more like a long putt than a full swing and you need to stay as quiet as you possibly can. Basically, only the arms and shoulders swing — the body does not really move very much. Concentrate hard on keeping your head still and the rest of your body will stay "quiet".

Avoid trying to take the club back in a straight line, as that can cause an out-to-in swing and it would be exaggerated on this short shot, possibly causing a shank — the ball coming off the club face at the point where it joins the shaft (also called the socket). You swing the club back naturally on the body target line, not the ball to target line. Look carefully at the drawings opposite and you will see what I mean. You must not confuse the body target line with the ball target line. The club is always swung on the body target line, never on the ball-to-target line. It is inevitable that the club will move inside the line a little on the way back; it must happen, but don't try to pull it in too much, nor try to hold it straight. As your arms swing naturally the club will follow.

Getting the distance right on this type of shot will take some experimentation — it is not something you can learn from any book, you must experience it for yourself. Try it until you can land eight out of ten balls within five feet of the target. You will have noticed that, as the ball is not getting very high off the ground it will roll once it lands, even in fairway length grass. If you were playing to a green the shorter grass and smoother surface would make the ball run further, so you would need to adjust your shot to land on the edge of the green and roll to the hole. For now try to land the ball short of the target, possibly midway between you and the target so that it will roll.

The next stage is to hit the ball further. The action is the same, but the back swing is now longer in order to generate more power. Again, think of winding the toy up; the more you wind it the further it will go. Golf is the same — wind the swing up more and it will release more power.

Stand a little more square this time, with the ball in the middle of your stance. Your hands are still slightly ahead of the ball so that you have begun the wrist-cock, so once again forget about this. There should again be an almost straight line from your left shoulder to the club head. Take the club back further, holding your head still above the ball and turning round the pivot. Don't sway. If you think you might, place another umbrella next to your right leg and avoid knocking it over.

As you take the club back further your wrists will automatically cock more — you don't have to worry about it, it's natural. Swing back about halfway, your hands coming up to just above shoulder-high and then through impact, again ensuring you accelerate through the impact position. You should finish much further through this time, the club reaching at least shoulder height. You will also be turning your shoulders more on the back swing and your body as you reach the follow-through

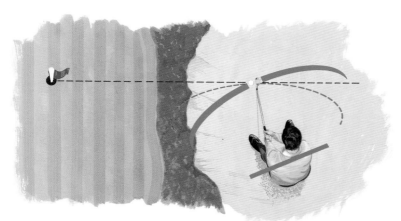

Make sure you always swing along the body line, not the ball to target line as that causes an in-to-out shot and a sharp hook.

position. At the finish there will be no straight line from your shoulder to the club head.

Earlier, in the section on hitting it straight, I suggested you should have the feeling of trying to steer the shot, driving the club head through the ball and on to a second target a couple of feet in front of you — we used a second club set into the ground, the shaft of which we were trying to hit on the follow-through.

It's worth reminding you of this now as you begin swinging a club and hitting the ball. We also need to go back to the swing path, where we saw that in-to-in would give you the best result. A number of players try to roll their hands too quickly as they hit the shot and end up pulling the club left too quickly. Feel that you are hitting through the ball, not at it.

As your swing develops you will increase the length of the shot simply by increasing the length of the back swing. Nothing else changes, apart from the set up becoming more square the further you hit the shot.

By now you should be hitting the 7-iron well over 100 yards and getting it reasonably straight. At present you are still only swinging three-quarters length, the club never reaching much more than vertical on the back swing.

Concentrate on keeping your head still and rotating your shoulders round that firm right knee on the back swing — avoid swaying; then on the down swing get your arms to straighten just before impact and then let the

This time, with 130 yards to the green and hitting a 7-iron I am standing just slightly open.

49

The ball is fairly central in my stance but once again there is a straight line from the left shoulder to the club head.

The back swing is longer, but still not full. Turn the shoulders more though.

At impact that straight line we had at address is replicated.

Not a full finish but turn the body to face the target as you keep swinging through the shot. Never quit.

straight right arm take control, pushing the club towards the target. As you continue turning the club will rise and finish past your shoulders.

One point I really must stress is that you began with that first little shot at a very sedate speed. As you increase the length of the back swing **the speed stays the same.** Don't believe that, as you increase the length of the back swing, you have to swing faster. The speed stays the same — slow but smooth.

A full swing with a 7-iron should hit the ball about 130-140 yards, but don't worry if you are not reaching that distance. Concentrate on getting a clean, firm, straight shot, the club coming down into the back of the ball and taking a divot — never try to lift the ball off the turf cleanly. Take a divot — it's the sign of a well-struck shot.

Any time your shots get out of control, come back to the essentials and hit short, 60-yard shots with the 7-iron. It will put you back on the right track.

You will also now find that the other lofted clubs in the bag, 8, 9 and wedge, become easy to use. They hit the ball less distance but higher, which is what they are made for. They are used to get the ball safely onto the green over bunkers, streams or any other hazards in front of the green.

Your set up on these short shots should always be the same. Have the ball in the middle of your stance, stand very slightly open to your target (more open the closer you are to the green) with your weight about 65% on your left foot, so that you are pressing the hands slightly ahead of the ball at all times. Take the club away smoothly, following your body line and try to keep your head as still as you can, using your arms and shoulders more to generate the power you need, always remembering that 45:55 ratio for the swing. Always guard against swaying on the back swing. Concentrate only on getting the club face square to the target at impact and leave aside all other thoughts about weight transfer, wrist-cock and anything else.

It will pay you enormous dividends if you practise the short game consistently. Even at a driving range, where the temptation is to spend all the time hitting the driver, spend at least half your time with the shorter clubs, always aiming for a specific target. At your golf course you may find a practice area where you can hit over a bunker to a green. If not practise chipping the ball over your golf bag, using that as an imaginary hazard. Alter the distance now and then, starting with the 7-iron chip and run, then moving back to use the 9-iron, 8 and then the full swing with the 7-iron. Always aim for a specific target rather than just trying to hit as far as you can. Despite what it might seem, golf is not a matter of who can hit hardest, but of who can work the ball safely to the target.

Backspin
Much is heard about backspin these days and on televised golf tournaments we always see the professionals hitting shots to the

Seve Ballesteros and most other professionals use balata balls, but they do need to be hit perfectly if they are to spin back. Ironically, most amateur golfers need to hit further.

green which then spin back towards the hole — and sometimes back off the front of the green.

Whenever you hit a golf ball you spin it. If you hit it with side spin it will spin to one side — a slice or a hook. If you hit it with topspin, as you do a wood off the tee, it will travel further. On a shorter shot you want the ball to go straight but high. That needs backspin and every time you hit the ball straight with a short iron you hit it with backspin.

Almost every golfer wants to get his hands on the magic potion that is going to allow him to spin the ball back like the professionals, but few actually need it, as most golfers leave the ball short of the flag anyway. The vast majority need to hit the ball further so that it runs towards the pin. It is rare that the club golfer goes through the back of the green. And in truth there is no magic potion. Getting backspin on the ball only takes a perfectly hit shot and a balata ball.

The perfectly hit shot is one where the club face connects with the back of the ball as the club is still coming down. That squeezes the ball against the turf and puts backspin on it, causing it to rise quickly. You will do that as you improve.

Balata balls are more expensive than the normal surlyn covered balls that most people use; they also cut easier as they have softer covers. Professionals change their golf ball about every four holes as they mark or even split them. If you can afford five expensive, new golf balls a round, then fine. I consider I have done well if I get round with the one ball, not losing any on the way!

I think Ben Hogan explained

backspin better by calling it "underspin" — that is by hitting under the ball you put spin under it, making it rise faster and stop quicker once it lands.

What you will find as you improve is that, when you hit a ball very well, connecting at exactly the right point and hitting the ball straight, with no side spin, it will, once it hits the green, stop very quickly. This will only happen with the short irons, though, from about a 6-iron through to the sand wedge and particularly when the green is wet and soft. Don't expect to hit a 3-wood at the green and have it stop on landing. Not even Faldo can do that!

Getting it on the Green

At this point we are going to leave aside the technique of hitting the ball and look at the important mental side of golf, as it relates to short shots.

There will be many occasions on the golf course where you are faced with a shot to a green that is not straightforward. There may be a lake in the way, or a large bunker, or the green may be elevated so that you can only see the top of the flag. You might have mis-hit your approach shot and need to get the ball close to the pin to have a chance of saving par.

The instant you are faced with such a shot you put extra pressure on yourself. New golfers in particular have a terrible fear of hitting the ball over a lake or bunker and as they face up to the shot they are more tense than normal.

It's easy for me to tell you to just

Put a lake between you and the green and the shot becomes totally different.

ignore the water — forget it's even there. When you're standing on the edge of a lake or in front of a huge bunker, that's not a lot of help. You can't make the water disappear and closing your eyes won't do you much good either. The lake or bunker is there and will be for some good few years to come, unless there's a terrible drought or they alter the course.

What you should do is to look at it from a financial point of view. The golf ball has cost you something and if you lose it you will have to buy another. If you do have to buy another ball, will it ruin you? Is it a case of buy another golf ball or pay the mortgage? If the financial loss of this golf ball is going to affect you, give up golf.

Set up with about 65% of your weight towards your left side, take enough club and grip down slightly for extra control.

If not, what are you worried about? On the practice range, or even on the course if there was no bunker or lake in the way, you would calmly hit the ball to the green without a second thought. To make extra sure you will hit the ball over the hazard, set up as normal but push your hands forward just a little more than usual.

Your weight should be about 65% on your left side. That way you are bound to hit down harder and firmer into the back of the ball. Hitting down gets the ball up. The only thing you need worry about is that you have sufficient club to get the ball the distance to the green.

For this it might help if you take one more club (a 7-iron rather than an 8) than you think you need and grip down a little more for greater control. Water always tends to shorten distances; and secondly that you have aligned the club face correctly.

The same goes every time you really feel you have to get the ball onto the putting surface. By taking extra club and gripping down very slightly you will increase your chance of getting the ball safely on the green. You should also be looking very carefully at the target to see where your safety zone is. If the green is long and narrow, for example, you risk missing it. Which side is it best to be on if you do miss it? Are there bunkers on one side that look very deep and difficult to get out of? If the green is on a plateau which side would

Hit down hard but don't try to do anything other than play your normal shot. Ignore the water. The camera crew here bet me a pint I couldn't hit eight balls across the lake without losing one. I needed the drink after that!

be the least difficult from which to play your next shot? If the green is an odd shape and the pin is cut on a narrow part, go for the "fat" of the green, giving yourself a better chance. Look for the safety zone on every shot — it always exists. Remember that you are looking to be able to play safe shots nine times out of ten, not once in a lifetime.

The worst shot you ever hit is the one where, the moment it goes wrong, you say to yourself, "I knew that wouldn't work". If you are driving your car and are faced with getting through a narrow gap you wouldn't try it if you seriously doubted you could squeeze through. You would find an alternative route. Why do anything different in golf? If you don't think you can get the ball where you want, you won't.

Try to avoid the negative thoughts that so often creep into golf. If you do miss the green, so what? Will it be the end of the world? Put it into perspective.

Later in this course I shall deal with the various short-shot situations you will encounter in golf from time to time; chipping over bunkers, hitting from the semi-rough around the green and looking to get the ball close to the pin when it is safe to do so.

For now, I urge you to practise your short game; always ensure you have enough club; and then play gentle shots to the heart of the green or to the side of the green where there is less trouble. Don't make life difficult.

Don't always go for the pin, aiming for the heart of the green if that is the safest shot, as here on a par-3 shot of 130 yards.

How to Love Bunkers

The average golfer hates bunkers. Professionals love them, preferring to be able to hit from the sand than from areas of semi-rough around the green. They know that from sand they can control the ball better. I am going to teach you to love bunkers.

Bunker shots are really quite simple and should present no problem to any golfer. Part of the difficulty, I suspect, is that if you do hit the ball into a greenside bunker, you are so disappointed at having missed the green that you are giving yourself negative thoughts. Until you have mastered bunker technique you will also be approaching the bunker with some trepidation, thus doubling your negativism.

Yet if you have played a shot towards the green from, say, 140 yards and it has gone into a greenside bunker, you have only missed the green by a few yards at most. From that distance it really is not that bad a result.

If you caught the bunker at least you managed to hit the ball virtually the correct distance!

Because the consistency of sand varies from course to course, and is affected by the amount of rain the course has sustained recently, you are likely to be faced with several different types of lies in bunkers. The worst is probably a plugged ball, but even then you can get it out safely though not necessarily into the best position for a single putt to save par. There are also sloping lies which can be difficult to play from. We shall deal with those in our second section on more advanced golf.

For now we shall assume we have a reasonable lie in a fairly flat part of the bunker, that its face is not too steep and that there is a reasonable amount of green to work with. In these circumstances you will get the ball out first time, every time, and will be able to get the ball fairly close to the pin with a little practise.

During a round of golf you are not allowed to ground the club in the sand before you play the shot, not even on the take-away. In the practice bunker I am going to suggest that you do make some marks in the sand to help you.

Most bunker shots are fairly short so we use the shortest and most lofted club in the bag — the sand wedge. Unlike the other clubs it has a wide flange which is lower than the leading edge. Hold up a sand wedge and an ordinary wedge and you will see the difference.

The sand wedge was designed by Gene Sarazen, the great American golfer who won the 1922 US Open at the age of 20, going on to win the US PGA later that year, and again the following year. He also won both the British and US Opens in 1932 and the US Masters in 1935. It was after that last major victory that he decided the irons he and all the other golfers were using for sand were not quite good enough, so he set about designing a club that, instead of digging into the sand, as a normal club does, would bounce through the sand and splash the ball out softly.

Laura Davies, Britain's top woman golfer, shows how easy it is to get out of sand first time, every time.

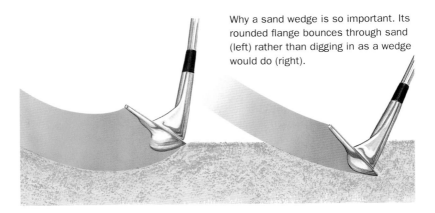

Why a sand wedge is so important. Its rounded flange bounces through sand (left) rather than digging in as a wedge would do (right).

The flange on the modern sand wedge does just that, making it the best tool to use if you are in sand. What you then have to realise is that you do not hit the ball but the sand an inch or two behind it. As the club bounces through the sand it gets underneath the ball and lifts it out on a cushion of sand. If no sand comes out, no ball comes out.

In sand we do not want to hit the ball but the sand behind it, so the ball should be central in our stance.

Remember what I said earlier about the ball position appearing to alter as you altered your feet alignment. Set up square with the ball fairly central in your stance, then turn so that you are standing open to the target — in this case the flag. The ball will now appear to be further back in your stance and if you look at it from the point of view of the ball-to-target line it will be between the middle and back of your stance.

You must align the club face directly at the target, not right of it as some golf books incorrectly suggest. The ball goes where you aim it. If you want it to go right of the pin aim it to the right; if you want it to go at the pin, aim it at the pin. One of the reasons for the misunderstanding is that many people refer to holding the club "open". What they mean is open to the body target line, not to the real target. Always aim the club at your target.

You can shuffle your feet down in a bunker to help you keep a better balance in the sand as the last thing you want to do is slide around as you make the shot. It also helps to remind you that this, like all short shots, is more of an arm swing rather than one involving the lower body. Your feet will only move in the follow-through.

With the ball where it is your hands will be pressed slightly ahead of the ball, giving a slight, automatic wrist hinge. This helps you to get the club up slightly steeper than normal.

With your hands ahead of the ball you will also have automatically put about 65% of your weight onto your left side, which helps to get the club

For a straightforward bunker shot have the ball in the centre of your stance as you stand square, then turn to an open stance. Your weight is more towards your left side, a straight line from your left shoulder to the club head.

coming down into the sand behind the ball. Do make sure, though, that your head is behind the ball. It stays there throughout this, and every other, shot.

Keeping your head still, swing the club up fairly high, at least three-quarters length. You must swing slowly, not trying to rush it. You must also swing along your body line, not the ball-to-target line. When you are standing open the body line is aiming left of the target and you will swing along that line.

That helps to bring the club face across the ball from right to left, spinning the ball as it hits under it. That is what gets the ball up in the air, and also what will stop it when it lands, which is exactly what you want. The steeper you want the

As you hit through the sand the club face is moving from right to left across the ball, helping to lift it out softly. Do follow through, not quitting on the shot.

Take a good three-quarters swing if you want to get the ball out. But remember to swing slowly and smoothly.

ball to rise, and the quicker you want it to stop, the more open you stand to the target. It really is that easy to adjust the length you hit a bunker shot.

A bunker shot is the same as any other short shot, the only exception being that you aim to hit behind the ball.

I have said that you should swing to at least three-quarters length. That may cause you some concern if you only have fifteen yards between you and the pin. There is often the fear of over-hitting a shot out of sand but if you hit behind the ball as I have suggested you will never over-hit the ball. If you catch the ball first, thinning it, that is a different matter.

The main cause of thinning the ball from a bunker is that the player has raised his body on the back swing, thus ruining any chance of getting back into the address position at impact; or has tried to scoop the ball up in the air, causing him to fall back as the club approaches impact. That makes the club hit the ball, not the sand.

Keep your knees flexed and avoid any temptation to lift your head as you swing back. Also avoid the temptation of trying to scoop the ball up to get it out high; again that only results in a thinned shot, or worse.

As the flange of the sand wedge bounces through the sand it will lift the ball out and throw it high. As it comes down it should, because of its trajectory, land "softly" — not running much but staying almost where it lands. You can thus afford to hit it fairly hard. Try it in the practice bunker if your course has one. As long as you hit into the sand behind the ball, you can almost hit it as hard as you can

and the ball will still stop on the green. This is only valid if the sand is dry and soft — if it has been raining hard it could be a different matter because the sand will be compacted and the sand wedge will not bounce under the ball but above it. Playing from wet sand is a subject I shall deal with in the second part of our course.

You must make sure you follow through to a full, high finish; never quit on the shot; never leave the club in the sand or you will have decelerated the club as it approaches impact. If you leave the club in the sand you will leave the ball in the sand.

To help you when practising, I suggest you draw a few lines in the sand as I have done in the photograph. I have first of all shown the line from the ball to the target, then the feet line and finally the ideal ball position in that open stance.

I also practise by just hitting at sand. Having drawn two lines about six inches apart aim to hit the club into the sand on the first line and have it come out by the second line. This shows that you are hitting through the sand and not quitting on the shot.

The vast majority of golfers who leave the ball in the sand on the first attempt do so because they do not hit through the ball hard enough.

Try practising with one of those air balls. They are very light and you need to hit the sand smoothly and follow through to a high finish if you are to get the ball out. It really is very easy.

There are occasions when you need to cut off the follow through to stop the ball quickly but I shall deal with that later. For now concentrate on hitting to the fat part of the green and getting the ball out first time, every time. It will do wonders for your confidence.

Before we leave basic bunker technique, there are two situations you may well encounter and I will show you how to deal with them. The first is the plugged ball, where you might only be able to see the top half of the ball, if that; the second is where the ball is in a fairway bunker.

Plugged Ball

A plugged ball is not normally too bad for it does show that the sand is not rock hard. In fact it often means that the sand is light and powdery, so you can hit as hard as you like. You do, though, have to hit down more into the back of the

For a plugged ball you need to be well balanced, take a three-quarter swing and hit hard into the back of the ball.

ball as you would for a normal shot off the fairway. Align yourself rather more square to the target with the club face square as well, the ball a little further back in your stance than midway, your hands ahead of the ball at address.

Take a three-quarter swing and hit slowly but smoothly. This can take some courage but it will get the ball out. Make sure you follow through to a full, high finish. Never quit on the ball when it is in a bunker.

Because you hit down on the ball when it is plugged you might find it easier to use a pitching wedge. With its sharp leading edge and no flange it will not bounce but will dig straight down into the sand. The club face hitting down into the back of the ball will lift it out safely, though you will not be able to control the ball once it lands. In these situations you might find it best to play to a safe area as I described a little earlier, instead of attempting to play straight at the flag, unless you have a lot of green to work with.

Fairway Bunkers

The other situation where you might find yourself in a bunker is out on the fairway. Fairway bunkers tend to be flatter than those guarding the greens, with no steep faces to hit over.

It is rare that you will be able to reach the green from a fairway bunker so your only safe option — and this is what golf is all about — is to play the ball to an area of safety.

Take something like a 7-iron, align square to your target — having chosen the spot from where you would ideally like to play your next shot — grip down the club a little and play the ball in the middle of your stance. Settle your feet securely but don't shuffle down too much or you will risk hitting the sand behind the ball. It helps your balance if you stand slightly knock-kneed.

In a fairway bunker you need to take the ball cleanly off the sand, the club hitting the ball first and not taking any sand. You could almost thin the ball and get it out.

You may find at first that you are taking too much sand so the ball will not go as far as you would like from a fairway bunker. You must resist the temptation to hit extra hard as this will just throw you off balance and result in an even worse shot. You are better hitting a shorter iron because the swing arc is narrower than for a 4-iron, for example. Remember, though, swing slowly and try to sweep the club through the impact zone rather than hitting down on the ball as you do on a fairway. It is a different shot and will take you some time to master, but you must persevere with it.

If you have a good distance to go — over about 150 yards to the green — I am going to suggest you hit the easiest shot you could. This is, however, only if you have a bunker with no high lip in front of you. In such a situation I would hit a 5-wood, and for two main reasons. Firstly, it will hit the ball high enough and long enough. Secondly, it will not dig into the sand but will take the ball off the surface cleanly, which is exactly what you want.

I have seen professionals hit the driver from a flat fairway bunker but that's taking things a bit far.

If you have a high lip to the bunker or are close to the front

You will find that the club digs into the sand more so you will not get such a high follow-through, though never try to quit — do hit hard through impact.

edge, this option might not be open to you. In that case get out of the bunker with the minimum effort, first time. The motto in golf is — keep it simple.

If you practise these routines and follow the procedure I have outlined in this chapter you will never fear bunkers again, because as you approach one you will know that you will get the ball out first time, every time.

Finally, as we are leaving the sand, please do remember to rake the bunker. If there is no rake try to smooth the surface with your feet rather than your club.

A continuing debate questions where you should leave the rake after you have finished with it — in the bunker or on the grass near it? You should leave it in the bunker, preferably as far away from the normal line of flight towards the green. If you leave it outside the bunker a ball could hit it and be diverted into the bunker. If the rake is in the bunker that will not happen and, should the ball lodge under the rake, you are allowed to move the rake without penalty, even if you dislodge the ball. Rakes belong in bunkers.

Above left With 150 yards or so to go from a fairway bunker, take something like a 7-iron and adopt a fairly square stance. Only take a three-quarter back swing as you must maintain your balance.

Above Your aim is to take the ball off the surface cleanly, with little sand.

Left Although you want to avoid too much body movement on the shot you should end up by facing the target, as with a normal shot of this length.

Right For a longer shot, and with a fairly flat bunker, I would hit a 5-wood, though you must be a fairly competent player to attempt this. The ball is swept off the surface fairly cleanly, though never try to over-hit it.

A Rough Time

Most golfers end up in the rough from time to time — some more often than others! When I first started playing I seemed to spend more time in the deep grass than on the fairway.

Even top tournament professionals veer off the fairway regularly as you can see at any tournament, so it really is nothing to be ashamed of. Nor is it something you should let get the better of you.

What I am going to do is to show you how to get the ball out of the rough first time, every time, just as we did from the bunker. In fact, bunker shots and recovery shots from deep rough are very similar.

The first thing to do is to go in and find the ball, of course, which is sometimes not easy, particularly if you play on some of the courses I do, where players have been known to go in looking for a ball and have never been seen again! Links courses are often better, unless you get in among the heather and gorse.

As with a shot which has dived into a bunker you must put out of your mind any negative thoughts, even though you probably have more justification in being somewhat annoyed about finding the rough than you should ending up in a bunker. Negative thoughts lead to negative actions.

Concentrate your mind fully on getting the ball out. You have hit a bad shot to go into the rough. Now work on hitting a good shot to get out.

I am going to deal first with very deep rough, the sort that comes up well over your ankles and probably higher than that. There will be times when the ball is so deep in the rough that you really have little chance of hitting it. You always have the option of minimising your losses by declaring the ball unplayable, swallowing the medicine of a penalty stroke and dropping the ball in a more friendly position. This is an extreme case and I hope it is only a sensible option in very rare circumstances, but if it is the only **sensible** option then you must give it very careful consideration. As I have mentioned before golf is about playing sensibly.

The first thing you should do is to find a suitable place on the fairway where you want to land the ball. Far too many golfers just go into the rough and try to hit the ball as hard as possible, without any real target. As we have seen earlier, on every shot you need a definable target or target area.

Walk out onto the fairway and see which position would be a good one from which to take your **next** shot. Always think ahead. Be realistic about it, not marching forward 200 yards if you have little realistic chance of hitting the ball more than 50 yards. Make sure that, from where your ball is in the rough, you have a clear shot to this target. If it involves hitting the ball

Even the world's top players stray into the rough now and again. Their first concern, every time, is to get out to a safe position. Their range of options is possibly greater than yours and mine, but follow their example and get out of the rough safely first time.

Left Check carefully that no overhanging branches will interfere with your back swing.

Right In deep rough your sand wedge could be your best friend. Stand fairly open as the club head will snag as you hit through.

Below As you set up your weight will favour your left side; keep it there throughout the swing.

out through trees, look carefully for low-hanging branches or anything else that might snag the ball or interfere with your back swing. Remember, your only aim is to get the ball safely back on the fairway.

Sometimes this might mean hitting out sideways or even back towards the tee, but if either of those is the only safe option, then do it. Don't waste shots.

If you do have overhanging branches on your safest route you might have to keep the ball low, but if it is in deep rough that might be very difficult. As I said, don't discount declaring it unplayable — you should never take two shots to get out of the rough.

Having chosen your target and your route, you may find that your sand wedge is your best friend, partly because it is the shortest club in the bag. With any overhanging branches likely to interfere with your swing that is a factor worth considering.

Your set up and aim are as important here as anywhere else on the course. On almost every other shot you aim the club face directly at where you want the ball to go. In deep rough the grass will snag the club and will catch it first on the hosel, where the club and shaft meet. This will pull the club

Hit down hard, your hands pulling on the club to promote a sharp downward blow into the grass behind the ball, in a very similar fashion to a bunker shot.

face closed at impact so allow a little for this, just as we shall do later in this series of lessons when we deal with sloping lies.

This means aiming very slightly to the right of your target, though not too much. Still stand square with the ball fairly well back in your stance to promote a steep, downward strike into the back of the ball. Your weight should be pushed fairly well towards the target, about 65% or so on your left foot. That sets your hands nicely ahead of the ball, recreating the almost straight line from the left shoulder to the club head that we had on short shots much earlier.

I would suggest a couple of practice swings first. This will give you an idea of how hard you will have to hit to get the club through the grass.

When you are ready, having chosen your target and your route, swing the club back up fairly fully and hit down as hard as you can whilst still retaining control of the club head. Pick the club up fairly steeply; with the way you are standing, the ball further back in your stance than normal, your hands will already be slightly hinged. It is that which will help you take the club away more steeply than usual.

As you swing down into the ball have the feeling that you are

Hit right through the ball, keeping the club head going or you risk leaving the club — and the ball — in the rough.

77

moving ahead of the ball, pulling the club head through the ball. You do need to hit hard, even if you do not have too far to go. Again, think of how we had to hit hard to get out of the bunker. This really is very similar.

The follow-through is still an important part of the shot, for it demonstrates that you have hit through the ball. Of course the long grass might slow down the club head and you might not have too much room to make a full follow-through, but you must not quit on the shot or you risk leaving the ball in the long grass.

Lighter Rough
Thankfully, not all rough is waist high and just off the edges of most fairways you will encounter an area of light rough. This presents a completely different opportunity

for now you have the possibility of hitting the ball a very long way.

Again, though, your first decision is to choose a realistic target. Because you are off the fairway it is possible that your route to the green may be blocked by a tree. In this case you have to take the easy option, hitting the ball to a safe spot on the fairway, just as before.

Look very carefully at the way the grass has been cut. If it is growing more towards you the shot will need to be firmer and you may need to allow for the club face closing as it hits into the grass. You will need to aim slightly right of your intended target in that case. You might also need to use a stronger club than you would use for the distance, say a 7-iron instead of an 8.

If the grass is growing towards

When the ball is sitting up, be very careful that you do not slide the club under it as that will hit it higher, but less distance.

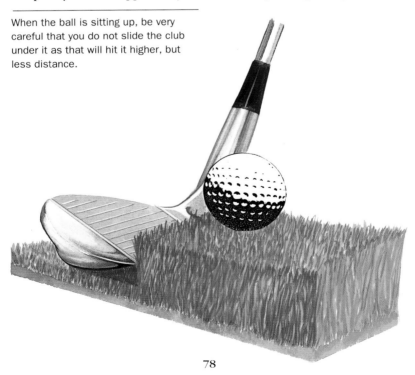

the hole you will have an easier shot but may get what is known as a "flyer", the ball not stopping when it lands. In this case take one less club (a 9-iron instead of an 8, for instance), and you could hit with slightly more of an open stance.

Another thing to look at very carefully is the lie of the ball. It might be sitting up high on the grass, or it might be sitting down, half-hidden. In some ways the second is better, because it will force you to hit hard and down into the ball. If it is sitting up too much you risk sliding the club under the ball, effectively skying it with a consequent lack of distance.

If it is sitting down, your set up will depend mainly on the shot you are trying to play. If it is short, just to get the ball out onto the fairway maybe about 100 yards or so, play it just like a normal short shot from the fairway, but as if you were trying to hit over a bunker. Have the ball a little back in your stance, setting your hands ahead of the ball, a good, straight line from your left shoulder down through your left arm and shaft to the club head.

Aim the club face at your target; if the grass snags the hosel it will only do so slightly so you should not need to make any allowance for this, unless the grass is wet or, as you take a couple of practice swings, you notice the club head is really getting caught up. If that is the case aim slightly to the right of where you want the ball to finish.

Have your weight about 65% to your left side and be very careful to keep it there during the swing, rather than moving too far on the back swing. Only swing about three-quarters at most or you risk

losing your balance. As with all other short shots, accelerate the club through the ball fairly hard, not slowing down but hitting through to a good finish.

If the ball is sitting up, which often happens when the grass is growing in spring and early summer, or if you are playing on one of the strong grasses, like Bermuda grass in the United States or couch in Australia, your choice of shot depends very much on what you are trying to achieve.

If you have a short shot of, say, 100 yards to the green, it is very similar to any other shot of that distance, but beware, as you risk sliding the club too much under the ball. You must keep in mind that the club will always find the lowest point it can. Thus, on a normal fairway shot you take a divot as the club reaches lower than the bottom of the ball. It will do the same here, so if the grass is an inch high the club will hit an inch below the ball rather than down into the back of it as it should. That hits it higher but reduces its distance. Very often you will need to take one or two clubs more than you think for the same distance, particularly if you have a bunker or something to carry to reach the green.

Stand with the ball about the centre of your stance; your feet and shoulder line could be very, very slightly open, though I prefer a square stance for this shot. Your weight again is about 65% on your left foot. Try to keep it there as much as possible throughout the swing, though as you will be swinging fairly fully it will not be totally possible to remain still. Feel natural, just concentrating on swinging the club up and down

The 3-wood from light rough — one of the best shots you can get. Treat it just as you would a tee shot, with a full swing and a hard drive through the ball as the weight transfers to your left, bringing your body round to face the target at the finish. You ought to be able to hit this as far as any drive.

and let the rest of the body react naturally. As always keep one eye focused on the ball so that you try to keep your head fairly still.

Hit through fully and don't try to stop the club.

Finally, we have what many golfers think is the best shot they can find — the ball sitting up perfectly in the semi-rough and 240 yards to the green. This is where the 3-wood comes in handy. You could even use the driver, particularly if you have a slight left-to-right dog-leg.

Treat this just as you would a shot using a tee-peg. Set up with the ball slightly forward in your stance, just inside the left instep. As you place the club head behind the ball it should nestle down into the grass so the top of the club will be about level with the equator of the ball — just as on a tee shot.

Take the club away smoothly and swing just as you would with any long club. I know this is an area we have not yet reached but as we shall be coming to it soon, in the second series of lessons, all you need to know is that you swing smoothly and slowly. The ball will come out easily and fly well to the target.

One tiny word of warning, though. A ball hit like this will not stop suddenly on landing, but will run for some distance, particularly on a hard fairway, so be careful that you don't over-hit it.

We shall deal with delicate shots out of rough around the green a little later as they are rather specialist type shots.

Get out of that! Nick Faldo proves his skills by recovering from a difficult situation at Valderrama in the 1992 Volvo Masters.

82

Sink that Putt!

Putting is the one vital part of golf for it is the only time you get the ball in the hole — unless you are good enough to be able to score a hole-in-one off the tee or chip the ball straight in from off the green. These rarities apart, you need to be able to putt.

More shots are wasted on the greens than anywhere else on the golf course. The par of the average course is 72; that should include 36 putts — half your score. Next time you play a round of golf, count the number of putts you take — make a little extra note on your scorecard. If you take less than 36 you are doing all right. Any more than 40 and you are in urgent need of help. Top professionals get round in under 30!

Very few people practise their putting sufficiently. If they did the putting greens would be as busy as the driving ranges. And have you ever heard of anyone taking a putting lesson?

A number of players believe that, as putting involves very little movement, it is not a skill that can be acquired and honed, as can bunker play or driving, for example. They are wrong. Putting requires skill and judgement, as do driving, chipping and every other aspect of golf. If a round of golf should involve 50% of your shots being putts, you ought to spend half your time practising putting. Very few people, with the exception of top tour players, spend that much time on the putting green.

The first thing to get right about putting is to buy the correct putter. This may sound obvious but you would be amazed at the number of golfers who do not have a putter which suits them.

Not all golfers are the same height and although clubs generally come in fairly standard lengths, putters do vary. Apart from those extra long ones — the so-called broom-handle putters — used by some professionals like Sam Torrance and Peter Senior, putters vary in length. Women's putters are often an inch or so shorter.

It would seem pretty stupid for a 6'4" player to have the same length putter as someone of only 5'4" but this invariably happens. I know the taller player has longer arms but even so, a longer handled putter would surely be more beneficial to the taller player.

Your first priority, then, is to buy a putter with which you are comfortable. Fortunately you can try putters out first, either on the putting green or on an artificial putting surface at a golf shop. My advice is to try several until you get the one you feel happy with. Try various lengths, and various head shapes. They vary in shape considerably and some of them seem to be designed more by modern sculptors than golfers. Many are heavier than others, which can be beneficial on slow greens but on a lightning fast surface a heavy putter could over-hit the ball. However, it

Payne Stewart, the popular American golfer, sends another putt rolling smoothly to the hole. The professionals spend far more time lining up their putts, taking more care on the greens than amateur players. Perhaps this is why they hole so many!

comes down to personal choice and, most importantly, effectiveness.

Putting styles vary almost as much as putters. Some people stand very upright; others are bent over almost double. Some have a fairly normal putting grip whilst others grip the club in a most unorthodox fashion. Even among the professional ranks styles vary considerably.

In this section, though, we are going to look at one basic method of putting — the one which the majority of teaching professionals the world over use with their pupils. Learn this one first. If it does not work for you then it might be time to try a few variations in stance and grip. More advanced putting techniques follow later in this course, but master the basics first.

First, as with all our shots,

comes the pre-shot routine, including the decision as to the length of the shot and the alignment of the putter. You also have to work out the slope of the green and to decide whether it is fast or slow. An uphill putt needs to be hit harder than one going downhill. A wet green slows the ball down more so you need to hit it harder.

Assume for this exercise that the green is perfectly flat, so we have no borrow to worry about. Very few golfers know the length of the putt facing them and whilst not suggesting that you pace out each one, on a very long putt it can be of benefit to walk to the pin and back, particularly for an uphill putt.

Having decided how hard the ball needs to be struck, the next thing to do is to align the putter head. You often see professionals these days lining the putter up in front of the ball and if it helps you then do it. The majority of players line up behind the ball.

Most putters these days have a white mark on the top of the putter head denoting the centre of the club and acting as an aid to correct alignment. Use these as much as you can, making sure the line points to the hole. As with other shots you can stand behind the ball to make sure of your line, though you cannot putt croquet-style.

Use the white mark on the top of the putter to help with your alignment.

An uphill putt needs to be hit firmly, more so than on a flat green. Obvious, but many golfers seem to forget.

Once you have the line, take your stance. Most golfers find it comfortable to have their feet fairly close together for a putt, but this is really a matter of personal choice. Don't have your feet too wide apart or it might cause you to sway. One exception is if you are putting in very strong wind. In those circumstances you may find you are better balanced with your feet slightly wider apart.

The feet alignment for a putt is normally slightly open. This will allow your arms to swing through unhindered as you strike the ball. In the full swing the hips turn left out of the way, allowing space for the arms to swing the club down and through. As there is virtually no body movement in the putting stroke, we need to create this space from the beginning.

However, the shoulders at address should be square to the target. Your weight should be very slightly towards your left foot, as you are slightly leaning towards the target.

Ball position is important. Ideally it should be a little forward in your stance. Your hands should be very slightly ahead of the ball, so that the putter shaft is leaning slightly towards the target. Once again there ought to be a fairly straight line from your left shoulder to the putter head.

Don't overdo this or you will not be able to strike the ball correctly. You do, however, need to have your eyes directly over the

You will find it helpful to stand with your feet slightly open for a putt, but try to keep your shoulders fairly square. I find it best to stand tall to a putt, rather than stooping over as some golfers do.

Your feet should not be too wide and the ball is towards the front of your stance.

ball, so if it is too far forward you will have a problem. Some players try to have their weight evenly distributed and the ball central in their stance but I feel this can often cause a putt which is off to the right, so I suggest you play it a little forward of centre. That in turn will cause you to lean your weight slightly toward the hole to get your eyes directly over the ball.

One more tiny word about the stance at this point. You will have seen many players stoop right over when putting. Bernhard Langer is one; Jack Nicklaus another. To be honest the taller you can stand to a putt the more chance you have of holing it. Both these fine golfers have suffered terribly on the putting greens during their careers though they have used different techniques to cure their problems. Forget problems — do it right.

Try not to bend over too much as it can affect the movement of the arms and cause you to miss putts. The important thing is to have your eyes directly above the ball. To check this get yourself into position and ready to putt, then hold another ball on the bridge of your nose and let it drop. If it hits the ball on the ground you are in the correct position.

You could also hold the putter with the grip on the bridge of your nose. If the putter head obliterates the ball, again, you are in the correct position. Check it, and check it regularly.

The most popularly used grip is the reverse overlap, which, as the name implies, is a reversal of the Vardon grip used for most other shots. It entails gripping the club in the normal way, then releasing the little finger of the right hand and the index finger of the left, and

Check that your eyes are directly above the ball by holding a putter between your eyes. It should cover the ball.

The most widely used putting grip is a reverse overlap, the little finger of the right hand and the index finger of the left changing places.

89

reversing their position, so that the little finger of the right hand is firmly on the club. The left index finger is then held fairly straight rather than curling round the grip. Holding it straight has a benefit which we shall come to shortly, though you can curl it round the right hand a little.

Now for the putt itself. There are two basic putting strokes, the "push" and the "tap". Some top tour players, like Fred Couples, tend to tap the ball, using a short back swing and a quick stab at the ball before stopping the putter head. This does, however, create many potential problems and I strongly recommend that you keep to the more widely used "push" putt.

In its simplest terms this means that the putter head is swung back and through at a standard pace, not decelerating as it impacts with the ball. The proof of a correctly swung putter is if the putter head finishes pointing at the target.

At address we have set the hands on the club in such a way that, when looked at from the front, your arms and the putter shaft would form a large "Y". The aim in putting is to maintain the shape of this "Y" throughout the stroke.

If you think about this it will become apparent that to maintain that shape your wrists will remain firm, not bending or cocking as they do in a full swing.

One way to get the feeling for this movement is to stand with your palms together in front of you, but without a putter. Just swing your arms gently back and forward, keeping the palms together, but making sure you do not bend your wrists.

If you keep your head still and just let your shoulders rock up and down — like a pendulum — you will understand what is required in the putting stroke.

When you then hold the putter and use the same pendulum motion, keeping your wrists firm, you will hole more putts. You should keep in mind the follow-through which, as we have seen earlier, is important in golf, even though it is something that happens after you have hit the ball.

On a putt the club goes back 45% and through 55% — yet again. By keeping the wrists firm — as we did on the short shot with the 7-iron much earlier — we finish with the left arm and club shaft forming a straight line. It must be the same on putts. Extend your arms through the ball, aiming the putter head at a second target just ahead of you. You should finish with the "Y" still in place and the putter head aimed directly at the target. This is particularly import-ant on a very short putt of just a foot or so, when you should finish with the putter head over the hole itself. That will ensure the ball is on the right track for the hole.

Earlier in this course of lessons we saw how the ball will always spin when it is hit. It is the spin that gets it airborne. On the green the ball does not spin — it rolls. It cannot be hit with backspin, topspin or sidespin. All you do is roll it. To get it to roll straight you will find it simpler to hit it on the equator, unlike a normal shot with an iron when you hit it with a descending blow.

Athough you address the ball with the putter on the ground, which helps you align the putter head correctly, you should be looking to strike the ball with the

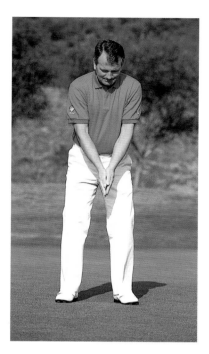

To understand and feel the putting "swing" stand with your palms together and gently rock your shoulders from side to side, like a pendulum, the hands staying firm throughout.

With a putter the movement is the same. It is vital the hands stay firm.

putter head slightly off the ground. In effect the putter is then rising as it strikes the ball, helping to roll it in such a way that it stays on line better.

You also need to keep your head very still whilst putting. On a short putt the saying is that you should hear the ball drop rather than see it. Concentrate on looking at the back of the ball as you putt, but then keep looking at the same spot until well after the ball has begun its roll towards the hole.

The strength of the putt will obviously depend on the distance to the hole, the slope and the speed of the green, but again this is not really something you can learn from a book — you need to go and practise. On the next couple of pages you will find some practice routines that will help you improve your putting. The second section of this course also deals in more detail with advanced putting techniques that are essential to lowering your handicap.

Before we leave putting, though, a brief word about sloping greens. If the green slopes from left to

To stroke the ball straight you will find it helps to hit the ball on its equator.

right between the ball and the hole, it should be fairly obvious that you need to aim the ball to the left of the hole, above it. The ball will follow gravity and the slope and, as it loses speed, will begin rolling to the right, down the slope. Judging the exact amount of "borrow" — the distance up the slope you need to hit the ball to get it to finish by or in the hole — takes time and patient practice. Much depends on the pace of the green and the angle of the slope.

Many professionals use plumb-bobbing to help them estimate the amount of borrow. I have detailed what they look for later, but it is not a foolproof method. Only time and experience will teach you, and you still need to read the pace of the greens. If only every green was flat! But then that would take some of the skill out of golf, wouldn't it?

Finally, please repair your pitch marks and any which less caring golfers have left on the greens. When a ball lands on the green, particularly if the ground is soft, an indentation mark remains. If left unrepaired for 15 minutes the ground will take at least three weeks to "heal". It can be repaired in seconds, if done immediately.

As the ball landed it did not push the surface downwards, but spread it outwards, just as dropping a stone in a pond causes ripples to flow outwards. To repair a pitch mark you need to push that displaced soil back towards the centre, rather than lifting it up from underneath.

As you do push it back in from the sides it will be raised slightly above the normal surface so tap it down gently with the putter head to leave a smooth surface.

Practising Your Putting Skills

1 Round the Clock

This is a good routine on a slightly sloping practice green. It involves placing twelve balls in a circle around the hole and then trying to hole each one. Any time you miss one go back to the beginning and start all over again until you can get all twelve balls in the hole three times running.

Start with the balls about two feet from the hole and, once you can hole every time three times, move back another foot and repeat the exercise.

You will find that twelve balls do not fit in one hole together so after you have six in the hole safely, pick them out. That makes you regrip and set up again properly.

2 One to Ten

This involves placing one golf ball about two feet from the hole and marking its position by a tee-peg. Hole it, then replace it, adding a second ball a further twelve inches back. Hole both balls, then replace them and add a third a further foot away and so on until you have ten balls at one foot intervals. Again you must hole every one of them. Any time you miss one start from the beginning again. By the time you have successfully holed six or seven you will begin to feel the emotional pressure you might feel on the course when faced with a crucial putt.

3 A Quick Nine

This is one I use when the practice putting green is fairly quiet and normally at the end of a practice session. Many practice greens have nine holes cut in them though if yours has less don't worry. It doesn't really matter whether you play six or nine holes, though I think six is the minimum.

Using three golf balls — use good ones for all your putting practice routines, not old, scratched or scuffed ones — start from any position and hole all three balls in two, that is two-putt each ball. Try to vary the length of each hole and don't be afraid to choose your own way round if your practice green has numbered holes.

For the three balls you should score six per hole, making a total of 54 for nine holes. The aim is to get round in "par". Think it's easy? Try it.